ABC···K

❧ SEOUL FROM A TO Z ❧

SEUTEPANIE LAPOINTE

SEUSEULOEDITIONS

KOREA **KF**
FOUNDATION
한국국제교류재단

The Korea Foundation has provided financial assistance
for the undertaking of this publication project.

© 2016 Seuseulo Editions
54770 Agincourt – France
www.seuseulo.com
contact@seuseulo.com

ISBN 978-2-9553877-1-9

Printed by Imprimerie SEPEC at Peronnas (France) – august 2016
Legal deposit: august 2016

Welcome to this illustrated ABC book which presents either the newcomer with a playful introduction to South Korea and its capital, Seoul, or the seasoned vet with some (hopefully?) humorous commentary on some accumulated observations.

52 illustrated words or situations make up this book in the form of 2 juxtapositions or otherwise ironic, serious, or less-serious comparisons per letter.
Creating this book was a real challenge, but it was really entertaining along the way!

AJUMMA vs AGASSHI

versus

When I first visited South Korea, I fell in love with the country and its habitants. Since that first day, I have travelled there, lived there, worked there, and made lots of close friends. And I always asked lots of questions!

My head filling with information, I started to collect my experiences by way of drawing every new thing I learned. Eventually, turning into a book became the obvious thing to do.

I hope that this book will help you to discover and fall in love with this wonderful country!

AJUMMA vs AGASSHI

The term "ajumma" is an expression which means "auntie" and is used for any older or married woman. Over time the term has become a stereotype to refer to what many consider the "third" gender.

After getting married, it has always been said that Korean women had to be strong and courageous to support their families.

You can recognize them through their appearance and attitude - they can be rude, pushy, and loud... but then suddenly act surprisingly friendly!

An Agasshi is a young and unmarried lady. Most of them spend a lot of time on physical appearance and elegance.

Their goal? To be married off by 30!

불고기

BULGOGI
"fire meat"
= marinated
beef

bbq

READY to SHARE ↑

← READY to MIX!

비빔밥 bibimbap

6

삼겹살

↳ SamGYOPSaL
pork belly

BARBECUE vs BIBIMBAP?

In Korea, you can eat what you want, where you want, and when you want it...
The country is famous for its barbecue (for sharing with friends), either inside a restaurant or outside in the streets.

Another famous meal is Bibimbap! This dish is made of rice (Bap) which is mixed (Bibim) with vegetables, meat, eggs, herbs, and gochujang (spicy sauce)...
Many different versions are available depending on the season, location, your taste...
Perfect to eat alone!

TiP N°2:
Both are perfect for those who don't want to eat spicy... (if you avoid the sauce)

카페 coffee

more than 10000
coffee shops in Seoul!

CAFES vs CONVENIENCE STORES

You can find all kinds of coffee shops in Seoul: cafes to relax in, a place to learn English, to knit, to have a fish pedicure, or to pet cats or even sheep!

And of course, there are all the international and local franchises.

As far as convenience stores go, when you are out in the chill of the night, on most any given street, you will be drawn to the warm glowing light of one of Seoul's ubiquitous convenience stores.

Open 24 hours, they sell everything from fast food to first aid products.

You'll frequently see locals shopping for milk in their pyjamas if you're there late at night!

24000 convenience stores in Korea in 2012

this one is a Korean brand!

Friendly Fresh Fun

GS25

Friendly Fresh Fun

tip n°3: Have your snacks and/or booze right at the shop! Lawn furniture "patios" abound.

ARE THERE MORE
CAFES
OR MORE
CONVENIENCE STORES
?
(the 64000 won question!)

In the Korean dramas, there is always a scene in a bus...

DRAMA VS DMZ

When I announced that I was going to live and work in South Korea, I was met with two different reactions, depending on the age and the cultural background of whom I was talking to.

Some responded by telling me about North Korea, the war, and therefore the DMZ; others told me about the latest Korean drama (television series) or movie they have seen.

A clear mark between the horrifically frightened, and the obsessively enthusiastic!

drama vs dmz

→ demilitarized and uninhabited zone running across the Korean peninsula, following the 38th parallel.
the DMZ is 160 miles long and 2,5 miles wide

tip n°4: visit the DMZ to learn more about the conflict

North and South are facing at the Joint Security Area.

E-smart generation

the E-SMART GENERATION
vs the 386 GENERATION

Korea is one of the most connected countries
in the world: high-speed connections galore,
the best international gamers, and many
market leaders in the high-tech industry.

18-25 year olds who grew up with this technology
and are seemingly addicted to their smartphones
are known as the E-Smart Generation.

386
generation

The so-called 386 Generation refers to South Koreans born in the 60s, who became very politically active in the 80s as university students, and were instrumental in the democracy movement of the 80s.

This was the first generation of South Koreans to grow up relatively free from poverty, and they worked hard to stimulate economic growth.

386 세대

tip n°5:
the term comes from Intel's 386 computer, launched in the 80's. Have you ever seen one?

awesome lanterns on Cheonggyecheon stream, near Jogyesa Temple

서울등축제

F

SEOUL LANTERN FESTIVAL

the Festival ends with a huge and beautiful Lantern parade in Jongno.

SEOUL FRINGE FESTIVAL

서울
프린지페스티벌

tip n°6: Outside Seoul, the Mud Festival in Boryeong in July, attracts many international visitors

FESTIVAL (TRADITIONAL) vs FESTIVAL (ALTERNATIVE)

Korea has an addiction to festivals.
Whether it's a traditional or alternative festival, summer or winter, in Seoul or in the countryside, there are festivals for any taste!
And they are often free.

The Lotus Lantern Festival is held annually in April-May in honor of Buddha's birthday.
Thousands of lanterns are hung up around Korea during this time.
The Seoul Fringe Festival is the most widely known independent arts festival in Korea, and is held every August in the Hongdae area.

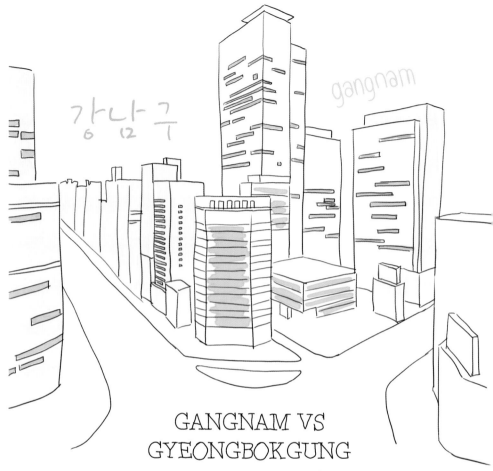

강남구
ㅇ ㅁ ㄱ

gangnam

GANGNAM VS GYEONGBOKGUNG

Gangnam to the South, and Gyeongbokgung to the North represent Seoul's two opposing faces: modernity and tradition.
The Gangnam neighbourhood is rife with luxury imports and modern buildings.
The Korean bourgeoisie and many celebrities can often be spotted in Gangnam doing business, shopping, or simply going out.

Gyeongbokgung represents the tradition and simplicity of the age of the Joseon Dynasty.
It is one of the largest palaces in Seoul and probably the most well-known.
It has many ponds, buildings, and statues. People come to relax in the gardens, but don't expect to see any cool old ruins - everything here is restored and kept in immaculate condition.

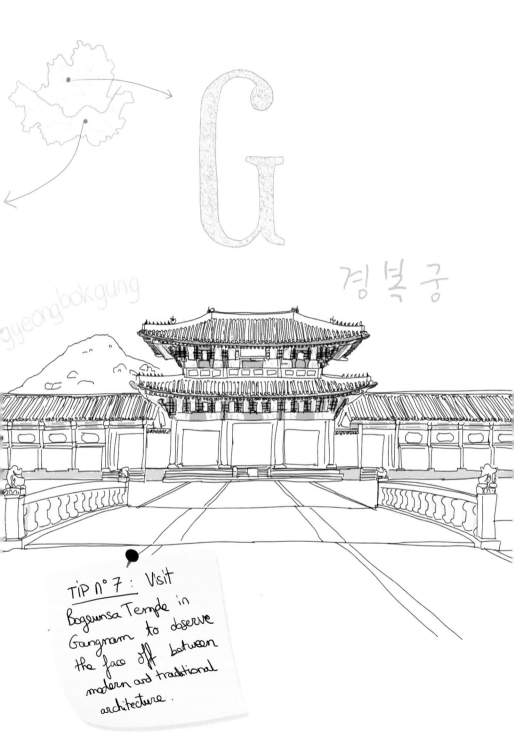

G

경복궁

gyeongbokgung

TIP n°7 : Visit Bogeunsa Temple in Gangnam to observe the face off between modern and traditional architecture.

tip n° 8: learn to read! the Korean alphabet is simple and could be learned in one day! Perfect to understand the menus!

HALLYU VS HAN STYLE

Korea is becoming more and more famous worldwide for its pop culture known as Hallyu.
K-pop, Korean dramas, and movies have millions of international fans and are one of the country's official ways of fuelling the image of an attractive Korea.

Given this rather superficial image, it is easy to forget Korea has much to offer in the way of traditional culture, and arts & crafts. Steeped in hundreds of years of tradition, they are the pride of the country. The term Han Style collectively refers to many activities deriving from this rich tradition: Hanji, Hanok, Hanbok, Hansik, Hanguk Eumak, and (of course) Hangeul.

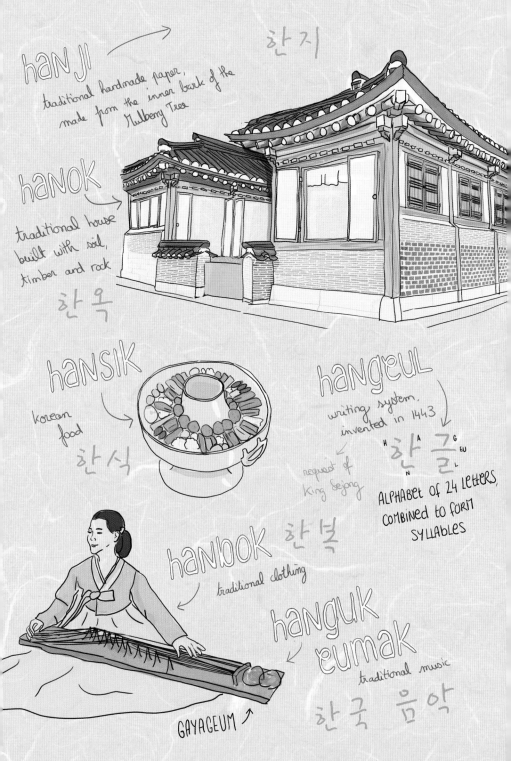

HANJI
한지
traditional handmade paper,
made from the inner bark of the
Mulberry Tree

HANOK
traditional house
built with soil,
timber and rock
한옥

HANSIK
korean
food
한식

HANGEUL
writing system,
invented in 1443
request of
King Sejong
한글
ALPHABET OF 24 LETTERS,
COMBINED TO FORM
SYLLABLES

HANBOK 한복
traditional clothing

HANGUK
eumak
traditional music
한국 음악

GAYAGEUM

tradition vs modernity

인사동

tea houses,
temple food,
Korean ceramics,
art galleries,
shops...

I

INSADONG vs INCHEON

Insadong is a traditional neighbourhood popular with tourists.
It is located near the Palaces, and is your go-to place for traditional Korean arts & crafts.
One big attraction for tourists is that shoppers can meet the artisans personally.

The airport at Incheon is one of the largest and busiest in the world, and is often rated among the best.
With its modern architecture and waves of travellers, Incheon International Airport symbolizes Korea's openness to the world, as well as its economic success.
All tourists to Korea will inevitably visit these two places!

인 천

tip n°9: Visit Ssamziegiel at Insadong to discover young designers — and if your flight is delayed, go to the sauna inside the airport!

how to warm up this winter ?

JJIGAE vs JJIMJILBANG

When it's freezing cold outside (those Manchurian winters!), two of your best options are:
- going into a Korean restaurant (there is always one open) to eat Jjigae (a hot & spicy stew), or...
- going into a Jjimjilbang: a Korean bath house with sauna, hot tubs, fitness rooms, and lots more. You can even eat there or stay overnight (as a cheap alternative to hotel).

찌개

A famous one:
→ army

(BUDAE) JJIGAE → stew

↳ originally made with leftovers from US Army soldiers when Korea was a poorer country: SPAM, Beans, hot dog wieners, cabbage, vegetables, noodles, etc...

찜질방

JJIMJILBANG

HOT TUBS   ROOM

before
meeting in the
common room,
men and women go to
separate baths...

tip n° 10: there are
several types of "BANG".
The most popular is the
NORAEBANG (Karaoke!)
If you are out with
a group of Koreans, it is a
hard place to avoid!

and even harder to avoid
the mic!

23

KIMChI

each family prepares its kimchi
before winter, during the

KIM JANG
↳ added to the UNESCO Intangible
Cultural Heritage in 2013

and let it
ferment in jar
for months
...

there are hundreds
of kimchi, made with
cabbage, radish, cucumber
... & different seasonings
scallions, ginger, garlic,
red pepper, spices, fish sauce,
shrimp sauce, oyster sauce.

배추 김치

cabbage kimchi
= baechu kimchi

radish kimchi

← The
STAR

KIMCHI vs KIMSHI

I always wondered why my co-worker kept calling his neighbour, "Kimchi, Kimchi...!"
Was it some kind of inside Korean joke?

Kimchi is a traditional fermented side dish, made with vegetables (most commonly cabbage) and a mix of seasonings and spices. It's an essential part of Korean meals transcending class and regional differences.

Then I realized that said co-worker was calling his neighbour "KimSHI" which means "Mr. Kim" and he was just being polite.

LEEUM (samsung)
MUSEUM OF aRt

HYATT

WHAT TO Do
on SunDay ?

→ upon my first visit,
there was a massive
statue by Louise Bourgeois
outside.

LEEUM MUSEUM vs
LOTTE WORLD

For many Koreans, Sunday is the day to go on a date.
A proper date activity is a must!
Museums, art galleries, and amusement parks are
really popular for this purpose.
Most places are funded by huge companies and bear
their names.
The Leeum Samsung Museum is a popular art
museum in Itaewon.
Lotte World is an indoor/outdoor amusement park
with many floors to explore as well as an ice rink and
attractions galore.

LOTTE WORLD

TIP n°12: during winter, you can also practice ice skating in front of the Hyatt Hotel, near the Leeum Museum.

ice skating!
← ice skating!
I want!

나가는 곳 ④
Way Out 出口

you can stop at a subway station and directly climb a mountain, even in the city center ...

tip n°13 : if you are brave, after exercise, taste the boiled silkworm pupae!

the most famous is Namsan

MOUNTAIN CLIMBING then MAKGEOLLI DRINKING

Hiking is a popular activity throughout the country, which has over 70% mountain landscape.

You will come across many hikers (often elderly) who are dressed to the nines in all the best hiking gear! Even in the subway these people are everywhere as there are plenty of mountains in the heart of Seoul and all round.

After a long day outside, nothing is better than sharing a meal and having some drinks. Magkeolli is really popular because it quenches thirst better than other alcoholic drinks. In the evening, beer and soju may also be enjoyed.

mAkgeolli

milky white rice wine,
made with fermented rice,
wheat and water.

막걸리

WHEN YOU DRINK,
YOU EAT ANJU → side dishes
like savory
pancakes,
fried tofu...

mAekJU = beer

← SOJU   25%

white liquor, traditionnally
made from rice but
sometimes from wheat,
potatoes...

Max

NAMDAEMUN MARKET vs
NORYANGJIN FISH MARKET

Do you want to buy fresh fish? Ginseng? Clothes? Spices?

There are markets everywhere which cater to any desire:

- From the most famous, Namdaemun Market, which sells everything in the heart of the city, and which has over 10,000 stalls.

- to one of the most beautiful (but definitely the smelliest), Noryangjin Fish Market, with its beautiful stalls of fish and seafood, there are also restaurants where you can eat the freshest fish you ever had!

SIJANG
= market

noryangjin

노량진수산시장

tip n°14: don't take the bus with your groceries! Eat them upstairs!

this is a bed,
spread it on
the floor

WHAT IS THE
WARMEST?

ONDOL vs OPPA

Which is more comfortable? Falling asleep on the floor, enveloped in the warmth of the Ondol (the subfloor heating system), or snuggling up in the arms of your Oppa?

Ondol, invented more than two thousand years ago, is present in all Korean homes and gently but efficiently diffuses heat through the floor.
This keeps apartments nice and warm in the winter. While today it runs off of electricity or gas, it was traditionally powered by fires which were either built in the kitchen or outside, and channelled through ducts.

Oppa is originally a term used (only by younger sisters) for "older brother" and has evolved to mean "protector", i.e. a boyfriend. A good Oppa takes care of his girlfriend!

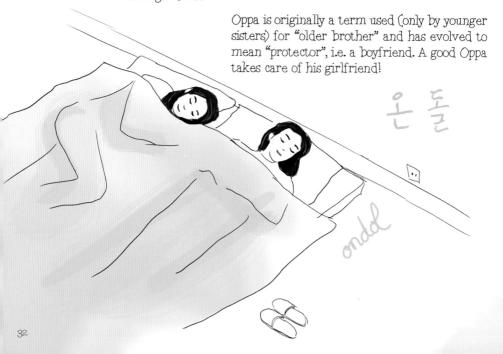

온돌

ondol

오빠

oppa

protects

carries her bag

pays

tip n°15: Don't be surprised if you choose a "Korean" (as opposed to "Western") room in a hotel and find no bed or heater. The floor serves both purposes!

there are always lots of flyers on the doors, many from chinese restaurants . . .

PPALI PPALI vs POJANG MACHA

Are you coming home late from work, tired, hungry, and in no mood to cook?
Either you take the time to stop at a Pojang Macha, a tent which can be found at night on sidewalks and which serves all kinds of hot snacks.

Or you order delivery, which will arrive quickly at your door "Ppali ppali" (quick, quick).

Even delivery is served on real plates! After eating, just leave them outside your door

빨리
빨리

ALL KIND
OF FRIES,
dUMPLINGS,
SKEWERS,
SPICY RICE CAKES,
KIMBAP...

rice and ingredients
rolled in seaweed

Some offer
more expensive
dishes and alcohol.
People drink there until late.

포장마차

POJANG

macha

tip N° 16: Koreans don't like to
wait — you may hear "ppali, ppali"
a lot — be on time!

«LES QUATRE SAISONS»
AUTUMN vs WINTER vs
SPRING vs SUMMER

During my first month in Korea, I constantly heard, "In Korea, we have 4 seasons" and I always replied "Yes, we also have 4 seasons," until I realized that Korea really does have 4 seasons!

Autumn is beautiful with many colors, especially in the mountains. Temperatures are often enjoyable.

Then it is time for very cold winter months with temperatures sometimes not rising above the freezing point for days or even weeks.

After winter, a beautiful spring emerges. Flowers grow, nature is splendid, the days are perfect for first picnics.

Then comes the rainy season (jangma), which is very hot and humid. This is the Korean summer, the mosquito's favourite season...Run away!

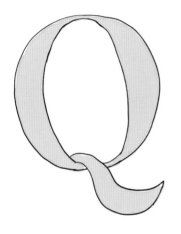

tip n°17: the best time to visit Seoul is from April to June and from September to November. Except if you like monsoon or snow!

Best Date at the Han River?

RENDEZ-VOUS AT BANPO BRIDGE
or RENTING A BIKE

If you are looking for some outdoor activities, you need look no further than the bustling banks of the Han River, which sweeps through Seoul from East to West.

27 bridges connect the two sides of the river, including the world's largest bridge-mounted water fountain, Banpo Bridge. Different displays are programmed every day, with lights and rainbow-colored jets of water dancing in sync with the music.

반 포 대 교

tip N° 18: cross the bridge by bike during the show...

There are many recreational facilities: pedestrian walkways, public parks, restaurants, cafes, sporting areas, convenience stores, and bicycle paths.

You can rent a bicycle with ease and ride for miles! Bring along a picnic!

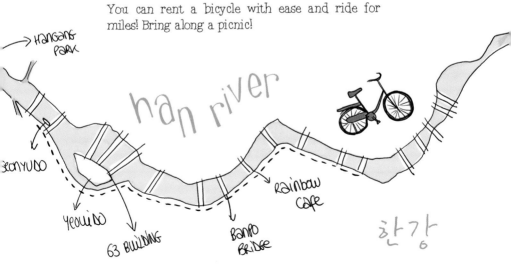

→ HANGANG PARK

han river

SEONYUDO

YEOUIDO

63 BUILDING

BANPO BRIDGE

rainbow cafe

한강

SHOPPING vs SPORT

Free time means hobbies!
While many will profess shopping as their "hobby" of choice, sports are also wildly popular.

Some neighborhoods are entirely devoted to shopping. Outdoors or indoors, you can find anything you want: international brands and designers, their counterfeit counterparts, and all kinds of fashion trends.
Many Asian tourists come to Korea to shop.

There are also many sporting areas. The most famous sport here is Taekwondo. It was officially adopted in 1955 and since then it counts more than 15 million participants worldwide.

↳ small crowded alleys at MyeongDong 명동

→ shopping centers, at DongDaeMun. 동대문

GOLF and BASEBALL are also famous

TIP n° 19:
You must attend a
Taekwondo show.
At Namsangol hanok
village for example.
It's impressive & free!

TAXI vs TRAIN

Commuting in Seoul is a breeze, thanks to their transportation network. The subway system is one of the best in the world.
The Seoul Metro is clean, always on time, cheap, and boasts extensive English signage.

When the Metro is closed for the night, you can take a taxi. Taxis are fast and cheap!
At night there are thousands of them. Some offer a translation service as well.

You can use one of the many smartphone applications to easily navigate transport.

you can pay with the same card, the T-money

tip n°20: if you do choose to take the bus, watch out: there's a good chance you'll end up on a "bullet" bus, which is one local term for a mad driver!

→ many lines, easy to use...

43

older sister, or older friend

Unnie, who are you?

UNI STUDENT OR ULJJANG GIRL?

For as long as anyone can remember, girls have always been told they have to be pretty to find a husband. Superficial beauty has become central to the culture, even to find a job.

Looking beautiful and innocent is not only popular, but the phenomenon even has its own name, "Uljjang". Uljjang means "best face" and describes a very cute person who has a saccharine personality to complement his/her looks.

But these days more and more girls are focusing on studying and careers.

Like boys, they are attending evening academies (Hakwon) throughout their schooling, and compete viciously for acceptance to the best universities, which gives them the best chances to get a job.

→ ewha is one of the most famous universities for girls

이화여자대학교

ULJJANG PHENOMENON
(Eoljjang)

얼짱

→ big eyes ⎫ thanks to
→V shape face ⎬ surgery
... ⎭

< I'm gonna eat
my milkshake
(little!)

No, I'm gonna >
eat YOU
rrrhh!

They love to take
selfies using cutesy poses,
to have aegyo = cuteness

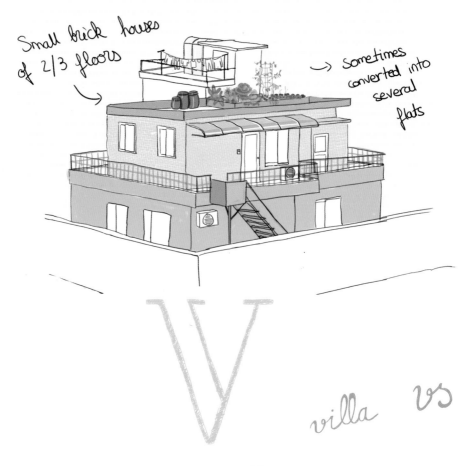

Small brick houses of 2/3 floors ⟶

⟶ Sometimes converted into several flats

villa vs

VILLA vs VERTICAL

Seoul is a city composed of hills which are covered by houses they call Villas. It gives neighborhoods the feeling of a smaller village, with a church at the top of the hill. The houses are sometimes rustic, but the view of the hills is beautiful. Above all, it makes for a very airy city with lots of courtyards and rooftop gardens.

However it is becoming more and more common to live in an "Appate", which is a modern, well-equipped high rise building, sometimes very technologically advanced. They are built by large companies and are grouped and organized by name and number.

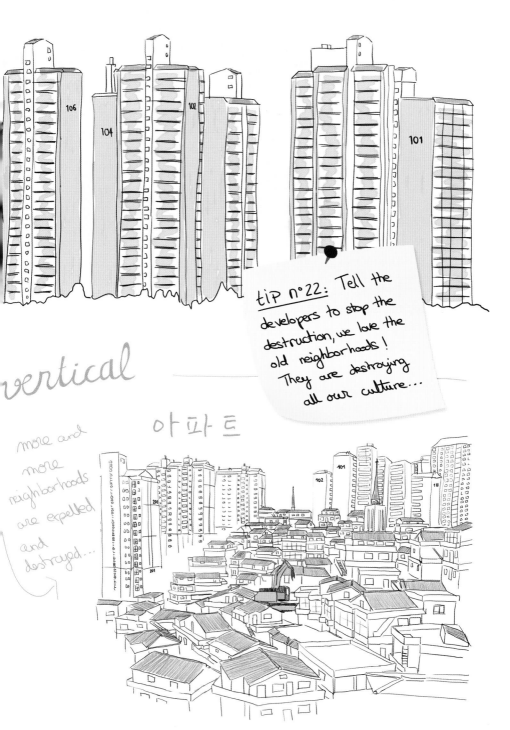

vertical

아파트

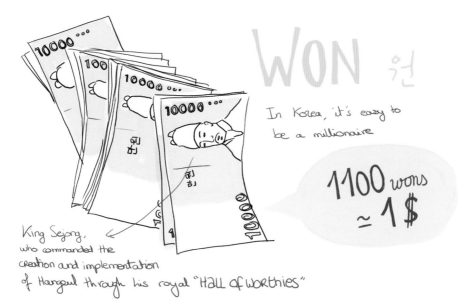

WON 원

In Korea, it's easy to be a millionaire

1100 wons ≈ 1 $

King Sejong, who commanded the creation and implementation of Hangeul through his royal "Hall of Worthies"

WON vs WIFI

What are the two most widespread things in the city? The won, of course, the Korean currency, which allows you to buy whatever you need.

And wifi! Everyone is always connected due to the impressive infrastructure, which even works down in the subway.
Koreans feel a bit lost when they travel to other countries without readily accessible wifi.

they are all personalities of the Joseon era

한국은행

오만원

50000

50000

→ AND THIS IS FREE!

WiFi

SHARE

와이파이

W

LOTS of MARKETING CAMPAIGNS ARE USING MOBILE DATA/WIFI:

- to transform a subway platform into a virtual supermarket.

- to organize games for people waiting at the airport
o o o

tip n°23: a smartphone is very useful because lots of things happen online. There are many apps for everything: transportation, chat, bookings...

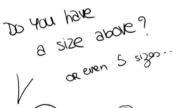

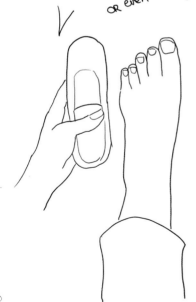

XXXS vs XXXL

In one of the largest cities in the world live perhaps the tiniest women in the world…

Korean sizes are very different from European and American ones! It is especially difficult for expat girls, as many Korean guys are quite tall.

It was hard for me (5'11", shoe size 10 - 10 ½) to find clothes in independent shops.
I had to shop in international neighborhoods, big chains, or online.

서울

XXXL

tip n°24: if you want
to have a nice view
of how gigantic Seoul is,
climb one of the mountains
which surround the
city ..

605 km²

→ more than 10 millions persons
(25,6 for the all metropolitan area)

TIP N°25:
- beautiful day: take a taxi boat to cross the Han River to Yeouido.
- dusty day:
Run to your home!

Y

the BEST & the WORST
in SPRING

the National Assembly building at Yeouido

YEOUIDO CHERRY BLOSSOM FESTIVAL vs YELLOW DUST

HWANG SA

It's time to hit the parks and enjoy the first days of Spring: The weather is nice and the cherry blossoms are in full bloom.

One of the biggest events in Seoul is the Yeouido Cherry Blossom Festival, on the island neighbourhood of Yeouido. There are large promenades lined with cherry trees along the river. Thousands of people come here to enjoy the blossoms.

But while Spring brings the most beautiful days of the year, it can also be host to some of the worst days - all because of a heavy yellow dust that comes from dry desert land in China. The air becomes visibly murky and polluted, and can cause breathing problems.

The two are unlikely partners - they will appear side by side on government websites on a per-region basis - the chances of beautiful flower blossoms or the chances of nasty yellow dust. Maybe both!

ZEN vs ZOMBIE

Two worlds still coexist in Korea: the spirituality, the zen, thanks to religion like Buddhism and the frenzy of modern ultra connected life.

Althought mostly young people are glued to their smartphones or their video games, you can still see very young monks who receive their education at a temple. It's definitely a country divided between tradition and modernity.

In 2011, the government initiated the "Shut Down Law", which prohibits minors 16 and under from playing online games (for 6 hours per night)

tiP n°26: discover also the other religions in Korea, like Shamanism which was the first in the peninsula.

→ they are also lots of Christians & Catholics in Korea.
Don't ever call a Catholic "Christian"!

index:

PLACES
presented in
this book

← Incheon

10 page 21

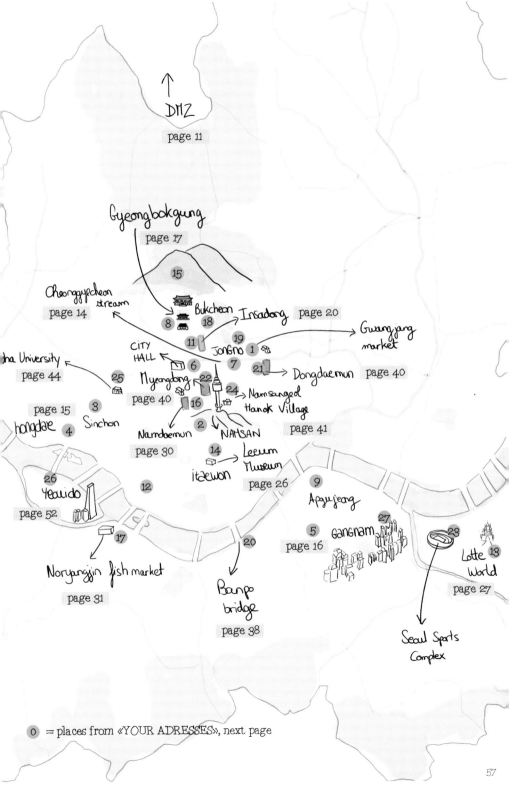

↑
DMZ
page 11

Gyeongbokgung
page 17

15

Cheonggyecheon
stream
page 14

Bukcheon
page 18

Insadong
page 20

Guangjang
market
page 40

8

ha University
page 44

City
Hall

6

11

19

Jongno

1

7

21

→ Dongdaemun
page 40

25

Myeongdong
page 40

22

24

→ Namsangol
Hanok Village
page 41

page 15

3

Sinchon

16

hongdae

4

2

NAMSAN

Namdaemun
page 30

14

itaewon

→ Leeum
Museum
page 26

9

26

12

Apgujeong

Yeouido
page 52

17

5

page 16

Gangnam

27

23

Lotte
World
page 27

13

Noryangjin fish market
page 31

20

Banpo
bridge
page 38

Seoul Sports
Complex

57

0 = places from «YOUR ADRESSES», next page

Where ? how ? → my suggestions !

AJUMMA > They are often in markets, as customers or sellers. At Gwangjang Market, you will share a nice moment with the seller, when having a meal at her counter.

(1)

Jongno-5 ga / Line 1 / exit 8   or

Euljiro 4-ga / Line 2 & 5 / exit 4

AGASSHI > Everywhere!

BIBIMBAP > A nice spot for Bibimbap is Mokmyeoksanbang, on Namsan's slopes. This attractive restaurant is surrounded by nature.

(2)

Myeongdong / Line 4 / exit 3

Cross the road in front of the cable car exit, and climb the stairs.
The restaurant is on the way to Namsan.

BARBECUE > Anywhere! Restaurants are always crowded in the evening. They stay open very late in student areas.

(3)   Sinchon / Line 2

COFFEE SHOPS > Walk the streets of Hongdae. It's a succession of coffee shops of all kind. You can also eat delicous desserts.
In the last one I visited, I met some sugar gliders!

(4)

Sangsu / Line 6 / exit 1

CONVENIENCE STORE > Everywhere!

DRAMA > You can easily see an ongoing shooting : at the airport, in the traditional neighborhoods or in students areas...
Some websites announced the past and present locations.

DMZ > Booking a bus tour from a company in Seoul is the way to go. It's a bit expensive but the visit is worth it and the best way to hammer home the notion that Korea is still technically at war!

E-SMART GENERATION > You can visit the Samsung showroom where the latest **(5)** models are displayed.

Gangnam / Line 2 / exit 8

GENERATION 386 > I used to see these workers every day in the area of City Hall **(6)** and Jongno.

City Hall / Line 2 & 1 / exit 6

FRINGE FESTIVAL >

Hongik University / Line 2 / exit 9   **(4)**

SEOUL LANTERN FESTIVAL >
On the Cheonggyecheon stream   **(7)**

Jonggak / Line 1 / exit 5

Euljiro 3-ga / Line 2 & 3 / exit 4

GANGNAM >

Gangnam / Line 2 / exit 8   **(5)**

GYEONGBOKGUNG >

Gyeongbokgung / Line 3 / exit 5   **(8)**

HALLYU > Around Apgujeong, follow the **(9)** «K-star road» to discover the places frequented by the stars and the production houses.
Start at Gangnam Tourist Information Center to get a guide book and visit the K-pop experience center.

Apgujeong / Line 3 / exit 6

HAN STYLE > While waiting for your flight, you can visit the Cultural Museum of Korea at Incheon airport.

10   Train A'rex to Incheon airport

11   INSADONG >

Anguk / Line 3 / exit 6

Jonggak / Line 1 / exit 3

INCHEON > Most international tourists arrive at Incheon airport and leave it quickly. But there are nice places around. Take a bus to join the beaches and the Islands: Muuido, Silmido and Sommuido.

10   Train A'rex to Incheon Airport

To the islands: from the Departure Terminal, exit 7, take the bus 222 to the Ferry Terminal.

JIMJILBANG > You can find a jimjilbang in any neighborhood.

12 The most well-known to tourists is Dragon Hill Lodge at Yongsan.
You can also spend the night at Happy day spa, in Hongdae, while waiting for the first metro after a night out.

4   Hongdae / Line 2 / exit 9

JJIGAE > Most of the korean restaurants offer some jjigae!

KIMCHI > You are going to eat Kimchi every day, but want to know more about

11 it? Go to Museum Kimchikan at Insadong.

Jonggak / Line 1 / exit 3   or

Anguk / Line 3 / exit 6

Or attend the Seoul Kimchi Making & Sharing Festival in November to assist at the largest Kimchi making festival.

KIMSHI > Trying ringing your neighbor's bell, there is a 50% chance their name is Kim!

LOTTE WORLD >

Jamsil / Line 2 & 8 / exit 4   **13**

LEEUM SAMSUNG MUSEUM >
The museum is situated close to Itaewon, on the hills.

Hangangjin / Line 6 / exit 1   **14**

MOUNTAINS > Lots of mountains are located in Seoul. I like to visit Bugaksan, **15** behind the Blue House (the President's house). Follow the Seoul City Wall to see splendid views of Seoul. But don't forget to bring your passport, there are security checks.

Gyeongbokgung / Line 3 / exit 3

And take a green bus 7212, 1020 or 7022 to Jahamun Gate Hill.

MAKGEOLLI > Makgeolli man, who sells his Makgeolli in the streets around Hongdae, is well known.
But if you want to try a good one, go to a specialised bar, like Danimgil Makgeolli Pub.

Hongik University / Line 2 / exit 7   **4**

NAMDAEMUN >

Hoehyeon / Line 4 / exit 5   **16**

NORYANGJIN FISH MARKET >

Noryangjin / Line 1 / exit 1   **17**

Cross the bridge and you arrive inside the market.

OPPA > Sorry, I can't do anything for you, you have to find your oppa yourself!

ONDOL > Sleep in a traditional Hanok, in Bukcheon.   **18**

Jongno-5 ga / Line 1 / exit 8

19 POJANG MACHA > Everywhere! There is also a Pojangmacha street in the Jongno area.

Jongno 3-ga / Line 5 & 3 / exit 6

PPALI PPALI > One call, that's all! Delivery to your door in minutes.

20 HAN RIVER > Go to Hangang Park near Banpo bridge. There are also many stations to rent a bike.

Express Bus Terminal / Line 3, 7 & 9 /

exit 8-1

Renting is free at stations like Oksu and Jamsil.

21 SHOPPING > Dongdaemun : korean brands.

Dongdaemun / Line 2 / exit 14

22 Myeongdong : international brands.

Myeongdong / Line 4 / exit 6   or

Euljiro 1-ga / Line 2 / exit 5

23 SPORT > Seoul Sports Complex contains many sport facilities, like the biggest Baseball stadium.

Seoul Sports Complex / Line 2

24 Taekwondo at Namsangeol Hanok Village

Chungmu-ro3 / Line 3 & 4 / exit 3 & 4

TAXI & TRAINS > Everywhere!

25 UNIVERSITY > Ewha Womens University is a famous university for girls.
Everybody can visit the park and discover the impressive building made by a French architect.

Ewha Womens University / Line 2 /

exit 2 & 3

ULJJANG > You'll easily meet these pretty girls in the luxury stores or close to the Plastic Surgery clinics at Gangnam, **9** Apgujeong.

Apgujeong / Line 3 / exit 3 & 4

VILLAS > Everywhere!

VERTICAL > Appate are built everywhere, but specially in suburbs and close to the rivers.

WON & WIFI > Everywhere!

XXXL > Climb at Mount Namsan, in the city center, to have a great overview of the city's size!
Take the Cable Car: **2**

Myeongdong / Line 4 / exit3

Or take the Namsan Shuttle bus 05 in front of this exit.

Or climb by foot!

XXXS > If you want to find Western sizes, go shopping at Itaewon, the international **14** neighborhood.

Itaewon / Line 6 / exit 1

YEOUIDO > **26**

Yeouinaru / Line 5 / exit 2 & 3   or

National Assembly / Line 9 / exit 2

ZEN > Why don't you stay one night at Bogeunsa Temple in Gangnam to relax **27** thanks to the Temple stay programm.

Samseong / Line 2 / exit 6

ZOMBIE > Go to a PC bang, to surf or to play online. There are some in all neighborhoods!

YOUR addResses

VISIT

BUY

YOUR addResses

WHERE TO EAT   WHERE TO SLEEP

A BIG Thanks goes to
Fenton
for his precious help with the translation
&
Hyeon Min.
Both made my stay in Korea a wonderful experience
...

Thanks to all my supports:
Francine, Sophie, Alex and the Korea Foundation!

스테파니
Seutepanie

SEUSEULOEDITIONS

www.seuseulo.com
contact@seuseulo.com